Write On Wirral
Anthology
2011-12

Edited by Gavin Chappell

DEDICATION

To all our readers and contributors.

CONTENTS

EDITORIAL BY GAVIN CHAPPELL

Write On Wirral was a product of Birkenhead Sixth Form College's creative writing course, which I have been teaching for some years. After a lecture on self publishing, some of the writers whose work is included within approached me and asked me if I was interested in setting up a magazine with them. We looked into the possibilities, and it soon became clear that an online magazine, or webzine, was the most economic alternative.

The notion was to provide a platform for writers from our own locality, and since the first edition, published in Spring 2010 it has gone from strength to strength, with many local writers seeing their first work published in its pages. In Summer 2011, the webzine changed from a quarterly to a bi-monthly, and we decided to celebrate a year and a half of publication with this printed anthology.

Within these pages, you will find works by such prolific Write On Wirral contributors as Margaret Etheridge, Justine Robinson, Carole Wilshaw, and Sheila Perry, who also provide our illustrations, and John Hoyland, a relative newcomer to the webzine who has produced some very impressive work.

To read more work by these writers and more, log on to www.writeonwirral.co.uk.

Gavin Chappell, Editor

MERLIN THE MAGICIAN BY MARGARET ETHERIDGE

Merlin the Magician – Myth or Reality?

Most people think of Merlin as an elderly man with a long white beard and a tall pointed hat, who was a magician at the court of King Arthur. But did he really exist, and if he did really exist, what was he like?

It is, of course, very difficult to prove whether Merlin did actually exist. Little or no records existed in the sixth century AD, when Merlin would have lived. Records that survive relating to this period (often referred to as the Dark Ages) only provide a passing reference to Merlin. Much later, in the 1130s, a Welsh cleric named Geoffrey of Monmouth wrote about King Vortigern. The king was building a fort on a mountain in North Wales, but each time the fort was near completion it would mysteriously tumble down. Vortigern's advisors persuaded him that in order to put things right, a young boy must be sacrificed. The young victim selected was Merlin. Just before he was to be put to death, he told the King that the problems were caused by two dragons that lived in a pool in a cave below the fort's foundations. The pool was found and the dragons released, which impressed King Vortigern so much that he made Merlin his chief advisor. Historic records show that Vortigern was indeed a king in the mid fifth century. A British monk called Nennius wrote a similar story, but the youth was not called Merlin, but Ambrosius.

There are various stories about Merlin's parents, but one of the more popular says that Merlin's mother was a princess who lived with nuns. When she was asked who Merlin's father was, the princess explained that she had been visited several times by a spirit who lived between the moon and the earth. On one occasion, the spirit took the form of a handsome man and left her 'heavy with child'.

It is not clear whether Ambrosius and Merlin (Welsh name Myrddin, Latinised by Geoffrey of Monmouth as Merlinus) were one and the same person, or whether Merlin has been based on

Ambrosius. Many myths surround Merlin; he was a magician and a wizard; he appeared as an old, wise man, giving his wisdom to four successive British Kings; he was known as the Wild Man of the Woods and he learned to talk to the animals. Merlin was reputed to be a mystical Druid, a Celtic priest, and Merlin the Wizard, the mystical advisor to King Arthur. He is also thought to have been an engineer, poet, necromancer, prince and a herbalist or physician. It was also widely believed that Merlin brought the Giant's Dance stones across from Ireland that now form Stonehenge. The medieval population knew and believed the old legends and myths about Merlin and he was especially revered as a great prophet.

One of Merlin's prophecies relates to an oak tree, which stood on the corner or Oak Lane and Priory Street in Carmarthen (South Wales). Merlin prophesised that:

When Merlin's Tree shall tumble down
Then shall fall Carmarthen Town

Other versions of the prophecy state that when the tree falls, the town will drown or flood. It is interesting to note that in 1978when the last fragments of the tree were moved to the Civic Hall in Carmarthen (Carmarthen being the alleged birthplace of Merlin), the following winter the town suffered the worst floods that it had had for many years and a train was de-railed!

There seems to be some grounds to believe that Merlin did exist, either as Merlin or as Ambrosius (sometimes even referred to as Myrddin Emrys). I shall leave the reader to make up their own mind as to whether Merlin was indeed fact or myth!

2 THE BATTLE OF BRUNANBURH BY JUSTINE ROBINSON

It was with the casting of the runes that the saga began.

The noble warrior cast eleven stones and fate was revealed. The warrior watched with anticipation of what was to be revealed. The shaman moved then stopped and shut his eyelids, after a silence the length of time for a bowman to withdraw an arrow from his quiver, load, and fire, his eyes sprang open and he told what the reading prophesised in a husky drawl. Despite its lack of volume, it was clearly heard by all that wanted to hear.

"Ur tells that you ask as you are challenged by what your fate holds for you." The warrior nodded and so the shaman carried on, "Wyfed tells that you are fated with an inescapable situation. While Thorn foretells that you bring great strength to your challenge. Daeg tells of a period of growth and improvement. The challenges you face are well laid as you will rise to meet them."

The warrior was charged with energy by what he had just heard but he waited to hear what was also to come. "Jara bodes of a time of a reckoning where fate has come full circle and needs to be met. Rad dictates that it met now. While Hagal says that the road will not be simple. The immediate future is cast by Yr, which tells that you are within striking distance of success. Wynn shouts of joy and fulfilment."

The warrior stood, fired by the reading, his confidence in his ability seeming to act as a shield. The shaman raised his hand and drew the warrior back to the runes to hear the fate that he would carry. "Geofu tells of the gaining of wisdom which will help. But it warns that nothing in life comes without a price, so in order to get the wisdom you will have to endure a sacrifice. It is this sacrifice that will reward you with wisdom. Tir tells that your success requires great energy." The shaman stopped and looked at the warrior before carrying on. "Your fate is that of success but at the loss of much of what you treasure. It is a short fate of victory which will dictate that you never rest or you will lose many of your gains."

The warrior left the canvas shelter and joined the others following King Aethelstan to battle.

The break of dawn had been shattered with the sounds of fire-charged furnaces allowing for swords to receive a cutting blade sharp enough to cut a man's throat just by him looking at it. Across the field could be heard the others preparing to cross their enemies with their swords. A meeting of man and metal, which would only happen once; for the blade would live on to fight again. the warrior would hear the bubbling of his blood as it spurted from his neck and mingled with the mangled mud of the field. The Gods were called and each spoke to every man, exclaiming his name. If a warrior did not leave this place as a victor then he intended to leave in the embrace of a maiden, taking him to spend his eternity with the Gods feasting on the finest food and drinking from the horns of magnificent wine flowing from the horns like the rivers run to the sea. With the finest bards telling sagas full of glory, of battles where the slain lay chopped and hacked together, so that only the maidens had been able to determine who was worthy of the eternity filled with glory and who was to be ignored.

The sound of animals split through the air. They had delivered their mighty warriors and now waited in order to take them back to their family as the victors left the scavengers to remove all wealth and weapons from the slain.

They stood waiting to battle. The energy and passion of even the lowest warrior was enough to jolt anyone close. The muttering of warriors ready to be slain for their country: for Alba, for Angleland, for Wessex, for Strathclyde, for Northumbria. For Victory.

As the single yellow star rose and split the dark of the sky asunder, the warriors charged, wielding the swords with the might that the gods had bestowed on them. Each warrior fought hand to hand with their enemy. It did not matter who was slain as long as the righteous were victorious.

The Angles were a united force, fighting for their country, fighting for control of all the isles. They had fought and won Northumbria and intended to collect the crown of Alba, of York and Dublin to be the supreme warriors. Shields were shattered by powerful blows, as their warriors became one with the ground drenched in their blood. The fugitives sought shelter but were hewn down where they stood; only the victorious would be left alive on the battle.

Warriors sent to eternal sleep under the stroke of a well hammered sword. The falling of spears further drenched the battle-scarred warriors with death. The ground was a mire of mud created from the gore of so many noble warriors. In order to flee from the swoop of a sharpen blade or the crushing blow of a battle hammer you trampled over your massacred friend and held on to your life.

Aching limbs do not move swiftly even when faced with steel and a hammer, though these did spur many on to flee the field. The men left behind men who they had known all their lives. They left their leaders, who had fought by their side and suffered the same onslaught of pain and fear. All those who did not fare well from their encounter with the weapons of personal destruction, were left to rot. For the glory of the scavengers, both man and beast, to feed off the life-stripped warriors sprawled over ground, which would be forever Angleland.

Once he had found his son, King Constantine returned to Alba, there to establish his kingdom as separate from King Aethelstan and Prince Edmund's land; so his noble warriors and brave people could be as righteous as he believed them to be. Olaf Guthfrithson sailed back to Dublin, to consider the battle a lesson well learnt and to work out what he would do next in his desire to grow more powerful. Even his marriage to Constantine's daughter would gain him no power as they had been vanquished to by a united force. Owen of Strathclyde and the Earls of Northumbria had no choice but submit to the rule of Aethelstan and give him the tribute he would demand.

For Aethelstan and Prince Edmund was the proof that they ruled a united state. They were in charge and receiving tribute from those not under their direct control. Many warriors had lost their lives to the tools of war. The survivors were blood- and gut-splattered, but they were victors. They walked away from friends who had chosen the wrong side, leaving the life-hewn bodies for whatever would desire them. The tears of their families echoed as a whisper to the cheers of the men laying claim to their lands and their families. The Battle of Brunanburh - a lesson to future warriors to make sure that they fought for the right side.

The toll of dead showed that the belligerence, and the need to be victor, always comes at a cost. For King Constantine it was the loss of his son as well as all his men and those belonging to his allies. His daughter was married to a man not entitled to enter the higher heavens till he repatriated his loss. Five kings and seven Viking jarls were killed in the bloody battle; their bodies lying sleeping under the annihilated bodies of their men.

The warrior returned home as victor but did not move with the swagger of the noble warrior that some would come to call him. He moved with the gait of a man who had fought filled with viciousness, and though not harmed physically by the weapons slashed and thrust, the images of the maimed and massacred men with the smell of the blood and guts gushing from their torn flesh would haunt his mind until the day he passed from this world.

3 PORT SUNLIGHT – WIRRAL'S HIDDEN TREASURE BY CAROLE WILSHAW

Port Sunlight, approximately three miles from Birkenhead town centre, is an urban garden village, which offers the visitor something special. The village can be reached from the M53 but the more picturesque way to get there is via Heswall, Brimstage, and Bebington. By rail, the local train runs from Birkenhead to Chester, stopping at Port Sunlight. A well known tourist attraction, Port Sunlight is a peaceful village and the apparent lack of tourists is quite unexpected for such a well known attraction. One reason for this could be because of its peculiar geographic situation. The village is enclosed, almost hidden, by houses and shops on two sides, a railway line embankment on the third side and the original red brick frontage of the soap factory on the fourth side, stretching back into a vast area of factory buildings. The road from Birkenhead passes the Camel Laird shipyard then takes you via Rock Ferry and New Ferry - areas of regeneration, currently undergoing major renewal and improvements. Another reason for the lack of tourists is that the Port Sunlight dwellings and public buildings are built around large expanses of green areas, recreational areas, and wide tree-lined avenues. The ambience of Port Sunlight is peaceful and tranquil, and somehow its spaciousness allows it to be undisturbed by day trippers - even coaches pulling into the car parks do not spoil the tranquillity.

In 1887 William Hesketh Lever (1st Viscount Leverhulme 1851–1925) a successful soap manufacturer from Bolton, Lancashire, began looking for a new site for his factory. The site needed to be near a river and a railway line for transporting the soap. He found his ideal spot and named the village after the soap he manufactured. Lord Lever not only set up the factory but also offered his employees a better existence and lifestyle than they would normally have had. Port Sunlight was built as a garden village following the same ethos as Bourneville in the West Midlands - though Bourneville can claim much greater fame probably because its visitors are far more interested in chocolate than in soap.

Whether Lord Lever's ideals were altruistic or not, this was his way of controlling his workforce and keeping them happy at their work. The beamed facades of the houses, though, give a somewhat false impression - the interiors are, although attractive, extremely compact and not all of the houses have gardens - many have yards and some share communal courtyards. It is well worth a walk around the backs of some of the houses to check this out. Whatever the reasoning behind Lord Lever's village, the fact cannot be ignored that Port Sunlight is a unique experience. Lord Lever encouraged recreation and education for his workers and promoted art, literature, science, music and religion. Many groups, societies, and sports teams flourished in the village and these traditions continue today, such as gardening groups, bowling teams, the theatre and music concerts. Since the village was founded, over thirty architects have built over 900 houses in total including some recent builds, mostly in mock Tudor or mock gothic style. All buildings are in keeping with the overall appearance of the village and local residents are highly sensitive to anything that does not fit the village tradition.

The Lady Lever Art Gallery is described as a 'national treasure'. It was founded in 1922 by William Hesketh Lever and is renowned worldwide. The gallery is small but it houses one of the best collections of fine art and decorative art in the country. It is a surprisingly light and agreeable gallery for such important works that entices the visitor back for many return trips. The collection includes British eighteenth and nineteenth century paintings, eighteenth century furniture, tapestries, and outstanding collections of Wedgewood pottery and Chinese porcelain. Two circular halls, one at each end of the gallery, are set with marble busts and sculptures, including some early Roman examples. The collections continue downstairs where there is an archival display of various memorabilia and commemorative miscellany. There is also a well stocked shop, selling books, prints, postcards, and gifts. The art gallery cafe is in the basement, where you can enjoy a snack or meal in the black and white beamed decor of the arts and crafts era of interior design. The toilets, off the cafe area, are not to be missed - complete with original decorative tiling and extremely noisy but efficient plumbing.

If there is time after you leave the gallery, take a walk around the village where you will discover many interesting buildings. The recently opened museum houses a model village and an exhibition of early photos. In the same building, there is a gift shop and a cafe (entrance fee to museum). Other buildings to see include a theatre (originally the men's dining hall); Christ

Church, the largest church on Merseyside; the village school; the factory building Lever House; a war memorial and several social halls including Hulme Hall which regularly hosts antique and collectors' fairs. The Dell is a sunken garden with shrubs and trees and makes a very pleasant walk or a place to have a rest or a picnic. For those with green fingers there is a good garden centre.

For families with children there are grassy areas for the energetic to let off steam, children's art trails, and worksheets in the gallery and a village trail obtainable from the museum. In front of the art gallery, there is a pool where children can paddle. For such a quiet peaceful area, sometimes the only noise comes from children having fun in the water, probably quite unaware that, like them, children from generations past have enjoyed this same pastime for around one hundred years.

4 A WALK FROM WEST KIRBY BY SHEILA PERRY

Introduction to Walking

Walking is good for one's sense of proportion, health and wellbeing. A five-mile walk does more for one's health than all the psychotherapy in the world and of course, it's good for one's physical health as well.

I once walked from Broad Haven to Amroth, which is 89 miles, half of the Pembrokeshire Coastal Path, a long distance walk of, 178 miles. I went with seven members of the Wirral Ramblers Association. We stayed in youth hostels along the way, which in itself was an experience not to be missed. The weather was very kind to us and some days we were sorely tempted to sunbathe. This was a wonderful experience for me as at the start of the walk I had been quite stressed out with work and at the end of the week and walk, I felt rejuvenated uplifted and inspired. A few pounds lighter with nice suntan, and a clearer mind, I came home feeling like a new person.

At the end of the walk, we visited The Boat House in Laugharne, Dyfed, which was the home of Dylan Thomas and his family from 1949 to 1953. This was a wonderful experience, an excellent finish to our week's holiday, with a slice of culture.

I am a lover of art, literature and history and walking can take you to some wonderfully inspiring places where poets, writers and artists have lived. It is so inspiring to be where they have lived and walked.

To be close to nature puts you in touch with your own mortality and to drink in the simple beauty of nature can be awe-inspiring.

I have been a member of the Ramblers Association for 20 years and during this time I have walked in many places all over the British Isles, Scotland and Ireland, and in Europe, everywhere there is always a hidden find, be it well known or just a simple discovery.

To love the feeling of solitude, the beauty of nature, the sky the sun the sea from all of nature's elements winter summer, there is such an abundance of beauty with each passing season.

I hope you will try some of my local walks on the Wirral and it will encourage you to travel further afield.

A SIX-MILE CIRCULAR WALK FROM WEST KIRBY VIA HOYLAKE PROMENADE, HOYLAKE STATION AND GOLF COURSE.

From West Kirby Station turn right and head towards Dee Lane with Morrison's supermarket on your left, head right along South Parade and down on to the beach. Walk along the beach following the track until you come to a rocky area known as Red Rocks with Hilbre Island on your left. When you reach Red Rocks, have a break and enjoy the wonderful view over to Hilbre Island.

Continue over the rocks turning right and walk along the beach and after about 20 minutes you will come to Hoylake Lifeboat Station and a small boating lake. Ahead are some gardens with a bowling green, further on there are tennis courts and a football pitch. The garden by the bowling green is a good place to stop for refreshments; there are benches to sit on and toilets nearby.

Return to the promenade, cross over North Parade and turn right down Deneshey Road. Cross over Birkenhead Road, turn left and carry on for about 30 yards, then turn right down Carlton Lane, and continue walking till you come to a narrow passageway on the right. You are then in Sandringham Close.

You should now be in a close with bungalows and a grassy circular area in the middle. Carry on forward through this then turn left into Sandringham Road. Carry on down this road till you come to a railway track. With the railway track on your left walk along this track till you come to Manor Road Station. Carry on past the entrance to the station and continue along on the track straight ahead. You will then come to a level crossing. Turn left over crossing. Go straight ahead for about 50 yards, turn right and follow the track till you come to a sign on your left for a bowling club. This is Proctor Road. Turning right follow the road round till you come to Newhall Lane. After the industrial units on both sides, it is a surprise to come reach the adjacent working farm on the right. After a field on the left, there is a sign warning of flying balls as the lane crosses the golf course. You are soon walking with fields to the left and the course on your right. The lane swings right and then left again to a straight stretch. In the distance can be seen the War Memorial and the Mariners Beacon on Caldy Hill. After passing a footbridge on the left and the small river Birkett, the lane narrows and the terrain becomes a little wilder. After you pass a small coppice, a board on the right shows your arrival at Gilroy Nature Park. As this board only caters for people walking in the opposite direction, you will have to look on the other side of it for the notices.

If you have time, a visit to the park will uncover ponds, paths and seats, a pretty secluded area, which I was amazed to find almost on my doorstep, so to speak. From the boards, continue along the main path to reach Gilroy Road. At a footpath sign, after turning right, you will come to a small tree lined village green. To its right is Coronation Buildings, which contains various shops. Turn right up Greenbank Road, passing a playing field, football ground and a hockey pitch on your right; you will then arrive at Anglesey Road. Continue along this road which turns into Orrysdale Road, cross over Bridge Road and just ahead of you will see West Kirby Leisure Centre and further on West Kirby Railway Station your starting point.

5 SOUL MATES BY JOHN HOYLAND

(1)

Sadie had fed the birds down by the marine lakes for over sixty years. Long before the swinging sixties and the Beatles, Sadie could remember the year all the soldiers swarmed down to the dance-halls. It was the year before the D-Day landings and the liberation of Europe. Yanks were everywhere. Down on the sea front walking arm in arm with a girl. Handing out sticks of chewing gum to the children that would congregate whenever they passed by. "Dew wanna stick of gum, chum," they would call out. Like many others, Sadie said that the yanks were 'over here, overpaid and oversexed.'

Sadie had her Bert and he was good enough for her. In uniform, with his thick mop of red hair, his eyes of china blue, he enchanted her. He was a little over six feet in height and towered over her. Yet there was no violence in him. He was a gentle giant of a man. He had a natural charm about him and along with his gentlemanly manners, he made the perfect partner at a dance. He acted from instinct when he held out his hand to her on the dance-floor or when he took hold of a seat for her when they sat down to eat supper. He had a quiet, thoughtful way about him; he also had a smile that melted your heart. When she saw him in the distance, walking towards her on a Saturday evening, she was so proud to be his girl she wanted to show him off to all her friends.

Sadie was a voracious reader. From the time when she was a little girl, she would always be found with her head in a book. Her father once said, give Sadie a book and the rest of the world ceased to exist. Ever since she could remember, she had been on the look-out for her prince in shining armour. He would rescue her from the dragon's den. He would fight demons and monsters for her. He would awaken her with a kiss; even lay down his life for her if that was the cost required. For Sadie, Bert was living proof that dreams could come true. He was her Lancelot. He would never betray her. He would be steadfast, even to death.

Often of a Saturday morning, they would go out together, walking hand in hand over the bright painted wooden bridge that led from the front. There was a faded gentility about the hotels there, all lined up, one after another, with their decaying grey Victorian fronts looking out over the lakes and the crumbling pier. It was as if they too sensed death in the air. Death that would come, without warning, out of a clear bright blue sky.

Bert loved to talk. Watching the ducks and geese swimming about on the calm lakes and the small sail boats on the horizon he would philosophise about life. "Have you ever thought that birds have their own class structure?" he once remarked to her. She was entranced by his words. No-one had ever spoken to her like this. No-one had ever asked her opinion about anything other than whether there was enough sugar in her father's tea or if they needed to buy some fresh bread and butter. Bert spoke to her as an equal.

"No," he went on, as if in her awed silence she had answered him. "Not many people do think about such things. But I do. Take pigeons for instance. Now they are you working classes. They are common and breed like maggots. They are just about everywhere. Then there are the ducks. They are the middle class. They always swim about in families, mum and dad and two little uns." "What about the gulls?" she asked him. "Where do they fit into your class structure?" "Oh that's easy," he replied. "They are the criminal element. They are the scroungers, the small-time criminals and gangsters, buying and selling on the black market. Then last of all are the swans, natural aristocrats. The blue blood of the bird world. They sit there in the water as if they owned the whole world."

Sadie loved it when he talked so. It was as if the two of them shared a separate alliance, as if they forged a nation made of just two citizens. Outsiders looked on but were denied the privilege of entering this world. People that passed them by seemed so mundane, their conversation so limited. They talked so intensely as if the ideas they explored really could change the world and make it a better place. He was the first socialist she had ever met.

They would talk books. He was a book lover. "Who do you prefer?" he asked her "DH Lawrence or Arnold Bennett?" "Oh, I love Bennett," she answered him, her face flushing crimson with passion. "He writes so wonderfully about what often seems ordinary. He makes the ordinary seem extraordinary. And what about that bit in Clayhanger when Edwin talks about the freedom not to believe. Why believe in something just because so many others do?"

They were both freethinkers. He had read Marx and Ruskin and believed that ideas could change the world. He believed that one day they would create a brave new world. "Some day money and social class will have no place. Then our common humanity will be all the bond that we need and we will work together to create a brighter future." Sadie loved it when he talked like this. She entered his world. It was sheer joy to be able to share their most private thoughts and dreams.

That summer never seemed to end. Never were skies so blue. They walked down Lord Street past all the stores and at night when the crowds would pour out of the theatres. They watched the wealthy patrons of the Arts as they stepped out onto the street and all the cars pulled up outside. All the lords and ladies standing there lost in their own private worlds. All that life of wealth and extravagance. There would be no need for any of this in the future Bert had told her about. Then all would be equal and money and wealth would be worthless.

A few weeks later, his leave was up and he was called back to camp. He wrote to her every day. He often included short poems with his letters. When she thought of how she had felt when she had first met him, it reminded her of a poem by Elizabeth Barrett. "The face of all the world has changed, since first I heard the footsteps of thy soul." The line had rung so true. His presence had changed everything. His absence left an immense void in her heart that nothing could fill.

He got a few days' leave at Christmas. He had bought her a book as a gift. It was a book of poems by John Donne. He recited them to her from memory. She was struck by some lines from a poem with the title Air and Angels. "Twice or thrice had I loved thee, before I knew thy face or name." It could have been written especially for them.

There was a sadness about him, though, a sort of melancholy she could not throw off. It hung above them like a kind of smog. Often they sat together of an evening, holding hands. Then they did not need to speak. They held a mute dialogue, which often said more than words could have said.

He went back to camp a few days later. There was something big that was going to happen. He still wrote to her but the letters told her little about where he was going. She received a birthday card on her birthday. It was the 6th January 1944. Six months later to the day, he was killed in action. He was in the first wave of soldiers on D-Day. He had barely gone more than a hundred yards up the beach when he had been killed by machine gun fire. He had died instantly. They had never got officially engaged but there had been a sort of unspoken agreement between them.

Bert's parents showed her the telegram. She could not believe he had gone. How could the world continue in its humdrum way? She looked at her parents and resented them for living. How could they carry on living when the love of her life was no longer part of the world? Everything seemed so flat and colourless as if all light had been bled out of the day. Food was stale and tasteless. Little seemed to matter. At night, her body ached. She so wanted to be close to him, to smell him, to hear the sound of his voice. There was nothing remarkable about the world she lived in anymore. It was as if a glory had passed away from the earth.

(2)

It was raining down by the marine lakes. The rain was monotonous beating a funeral drum roll off the two wooden bridges that spanned both lakes and the cold grey marble walls down by the old Victorian shelters. Sadie sat huddled in one of these shelters and watched the ducks in their pathetic attempts to shelter from the storm.

Sadie had been coming down to the lakes for weeks. Here she found some consolation. Here was the last place they had walked together. Here they had shared their last few days together. It was as if any moment he would come walking over that tired wooden bridge. For a while at least, she could pretend that he still was the vibrant young man full of ideas and wondrous thoughts. She walked by the lake and if she stood still and closed her eyes then he was with her, a presence still in her heart and in her mind.

She had taken to feeding the birds out on the lake. One morning she had found a duckling with a broken wing. Her heart went out to the damaged creature. It was like a symbol of her own damaged self. She took the bird home and nursed it back to health. She took bread down to the lakes every morning and fed the birds. She recalled Bert's words about the birds. She would sit watching them for hours, calling out to them as if they were kindred spirits.

Another time she found that one of the two swans on the lake had died. Only the male swan carried on, lost and alone, searching for his lost soul-mate. She felt his pain as he slowly swam about the lake, locked inside his private world of grief and pain. He was still young and proud and vain. Yet he had lost the compass of his heart and now swam directionless, wandering about the lake without purpose. Her heart went out to this noble creature and the pain she imagined he felt. Perhaps the spirit of his mate swam alongside and was a comfort when the rains came down and the cold nights drew in.

So she became known as the Bird Lady. Always down by the lakes. Always looking out for the birds, feeding them, consoling them, calling out to them. A strange little old lady, many strangers said of her. A little crazed in the head. But locals made allowances for her, and remembered her loss, and thought, there but for the grace of God…

The birds adopted her and would swim to the lakeside and come to her when she called. Even the gulls came to eat the bread she broke and took it from her hands with a gentleness that gulls rarely show. This lady was different. She was a deity of their domain, always there, week after week, month after month, in all weather.

One day in the summer of 2007, she was as usual down by the lakes feeding the birds when she spotted a young man sitting in one of the archaic shelters, reading. She looked at the book he was reading. It was Clayhanger by Arnold Bennett. "What do you make of the book you are reading?" she asked him. "Oh, I think this is wonderful," he replied. "He seems to have a knack of making the ordinary, everyday, humdrum world, alive and gleaming. He makes the routine lives we lead, extraordinary."

This was all the invitation Sadie needed. Soon they were on intimate terms and she was sharing confidences with him she had told no-one in over sixty years. They both shared a passion for talking about books and when he revealed to her that he was a writer struggling to write his first novel, she knew that this was someone she could open her heart to. So she told him about Bert and the love they shared and the life they might have had if he had lived. In going over her memories, Sadie was able to see just how blessed she had been. Even the short time she had spent with Bert had been more than some people found in a lifetime.

Everyday they met up. He watched while she fed the birds. Then they sat together and ate lunch or he read to her out of the book he was reading. Sometimes it was a novel, sometimes it was poetry. It was the sharing that brought her back to life. For her that summer was to be the happiest she had lived in a long time. She was no longer an old woman and all the hope and beauty of her youth came back in the talks they shared. He was lonely too and despite the difference in their ages, they forged an affinity between them. Their minds were both receptive and they shared ideas as they sat and ate their sandwiches together.

A few weeks later Sadie died. She had been sitting in the shelter. It was a warm day, with a bright blue sky. She had been waiting for the young writer. It was then she had a heart attack. When the writer arrived, she was still sitting there. She seemed so peaceful as if she had just closed her eyes and drifted off to sleep. Out on the lake two swans were swimming. The swans stayed close, side by side, as if one swan was a mirror image of the other. Their heads were bowed as if in silent prayer.

The writer sat with her a while. He took her hand in his. It still seemed warm. Maybe if he called her name. Perhaps even a kiss would awaken her from her deep sleep. Then as he looked up, he saw two figures walk towards him. A tall man in uniform, with a thick mop of red hair. Walking along side a young woman, dark shoulder length brown hair. Something about the clothes they wore that seemed dated. It was as if they were wearing period costume. It was like a scene from an old war-time movie.

As they walked past the female looked toward him and smiled. It was a smile that said everything. It said things are as they are meant to be. That enigmatic smile contained all the mystery of life. Then the two figures seemed to fade into the distance and there were only the lakes and the birds, oh so many birds on the lake. Among them the two swans side by side moved by with a breathless majesty. There was a hushed stillness in the air as if the curtains were waiting to rise on an empty stage.

The writer stood up. Leaving the figure almost sleeping on the bench he stepped down and headed for the bridge back to the life he had led. He had a new tale to write and he was eager to begin. He had much to think about before he began. Slowly he walked off into the distance, a sadder but wiser man. All the world was before him and the mystery of his life was only just beginning.

6 MOTHER REDCAP'S TREASURE BY GAVIN CHAPPELL

Pirate Gold and Smugglers' Tunnels.

We've all heard rumours of Wirral's piratical past and its connection with smuggling in the eighteenth century. Many have heard of Mother Redcap and the legendary smugglers' tunnels beneath Wallasey. Mother Redcap's death, however, enshrines a mystery; a £50, 000 privateers' prize had been entrusted to her care, but after she died, it was never seen again. Whatever happened to Mother Redcap's treasure? Was it spirited away into the labyrinth of tunnels riddling Wallasey's bedrock? GAVIN CHAPPELL reports on what little is know of the lost treasure of Mother Redcap...

Part One – Mother Redcap's Treasure

In the eighteenth and early nineteenth century, Wallasey gained a reputation as a haunt of smugglers and pirates. The centre of local smuggling was Mother Redcap's, a tavern that once stood on what is now Egremont Promenade. It was nicknamed Mother Redcap's after its proprietor, an elderly lady called Poll Jones, who always wore a red cap or bonnet. Mother Redcap was a great friend to smugglers and privateers, gaining a reputation as the "foster mother of wild spirits." The tavern was rebuilt as both a hiding place for smuggled goods, and a potential death-trap for unwary customs men.

Mother Redcap herself was very likeable, and assisted sailors by acting as a banker, minding their earnings while they were at sea. Many of the clientele came from the crews of privateers who anchored at Red Bets, the anchorage just opposite the tavern. Mother Redcap's was built of red free-stone, and the walls were practically three feet thick. Smugglers hid contraband in the walls and ceilings of lower rooms. Thick planks of wood from wrecked ships covered the walls. There was a front door made of five inch thick oak, studded with iron nails, and seems to have had several sliding bars across the inside. Just inside the door was a trapdoor leading down to the cellar under the north room, a rough wooden lid with hinges and shackles. If an intruder forced the front door, this would withdraw the bolt of the trapdoor, precipitating the unwelcome visitor into the cellar, eight or nine feet below. It was also used for the more mundane purpose of depositing goods.

If a visitor had successfully negotiated this initial obstacle, they would have the options of entering a room to the north or another to the south (although this entrance would be covered by the open front door), or going straight up a staircase directly ahead of the door. The main entrance into the cellar was behind this staircase, where seven or eight steps led down. At the top of the cellar steps, a narrow doorway led out into the yard at the back.

The beams in the two main rooms of the house were made of oak, and the chimney breasts were very large inside. There were cavities near the ceiling, over the oak beams that had removable entrances from the top of the chimney breasts inside the flues. In the south room was a small cavity, just large enough to conceal a small man. In the wall were other smaller cavities where Mother Redcap kept the earnings and prize money of privateer crews while they were at sea.

In the yard was a well, twelve foot deep, dry, and partly filled in with earth. On the west side of the wall of the well (facing inland) there was a hole that seemed to lead into the garden but probably led to a mysterious passage.

At the south end of the house, there was another cave or cellar, and a mosaic was placed over sandstone flags that covered this cavity. A square hole with steps, made to look like a dry pit well, was the entrance to this cellar. Much of the yard seems to have been hollow, flagstones on beams covering a large subterranean space. A manure heap and a stock of coal were piled on top of it; the coal was brought in small boats called "flats" and Mother Redcap sold it to the people of Liscard. When contraband was concealed inside the cave, the coal and barrels were moved to cover the entrance.

At the end of the cave was the mysterious passage mentioned above. Some sources state that it led to the Yellow Noses, over a mile away in what is now New Brighton, and also that another passage went to Birkenhead Priory. More conservative accounts say that it led to an opening in a ditch that led to a pit about halfway up what is now Lincoln Drive, in the direction of Liscard. On the edge of this pit grew a willow tree, which was used as a lookout post from which one of Mother Redcap's confederates could survey the whole entrance to the Mersey.

Mother Redcap had hiding places for any number of fugitive sailors, and of course she also acted as a banker, keeping the men's earnings and prize-money concealed about the building, and it was said that she had enormous amounts of money concealed, but its location was never revealed. It is said that shortly before her death a privateer ship came into port in Liverpool with a fabulously rich prize that had given the crew at least £1, 000 (£50, 000 in today's money) each. Mother Redcap's was "swarming" with sailors from this ship, and she received a great deal of the prize-money for safekeeping. She died soon after, and little property was found in her possession. The location of the privateers' prize money remains a mystery to this day.

After Mother Redcap's death, the tavern continued to be an important landmark, even after it had had its license revoked. A retired solicitor called Joseph Kitchingham bought it in 1888, restoring and renovating the building, adding a turret attic, a further wing and various enlargements and alterations, including a date plate inscribed with the legend 1595 – 1889. The property was sold after Kitchingham's death when it was bought by Robert Myles who opened it as a café, named Mother Redcap's Café.

By the 1950s, the house had come into the possession of the Grimshaw family, whose son Wolfgang was a childhood friend of local historian Joseph "Pepe" Ruiz. In the latter's book "Beachcombers, Buttercreams and Smuggler's Caves" he relates his experiences of the building in its later years. Digging in the south west corner the two boys got down no more than a foot before their spades met a large sandstone slab, which further excavations revealed to be part of a set of steps leading downwards.

Mother Redcap's was never a success as a café. It also failed as a nightclub – the aptly-named Galleon Club -- and closed in 1960, falling into ruin before being demolished in October 1974. Joseph Ruiz records that during the demolition a bulldozer fell through a hole in the ground, revealing a large well with an entrance door part of the way down. The workers recognised this as the famous "smugglers' well" and one man suggested his mates lower him down to the door and they inform the museum authorities. The foreman, however, insisted that the well be filled in, and threatened instant dismissal to anyone contacting the museum. Mother Redcap's secrets were finally buried. Soon after, a nursing home was built on the site, and it still stands today.

Part Two – Smugglers' Tunnels

A 1974 article in the Wirral News stated that the developers found no trace of tunnels while building the nursing home on the site of Mother Redcap's. However, Joan McCool of Rivington Road, who had worked at the Galleon Club in the fifties, said that behind the bar there had been a large bank with several tunnels that had been partially filled in with beer bottles. To the left of the bar there was a large slit, which would go unnoticed unless drawn to a visitor's attention. This could be entered sideways, and led to a black, damp tunnel running behind the bar and seeming to go on much further.

Inga Kneale, the Galleon Club's former proprietor, said that although she had never found tunnels "of any length" she was sure that they existed, and had always felt that someone was watching her. A previous owner had excavated the dance floor while searching for the passages, but had been unsuccessful. A geo-physical survey in the mid seventies by Ezekiel Palmer of the Proudman Institute also failed to reveal any sign of tunnels.

However, a letter from Marion Fisher, former owner of an hotel in Wellington Road, mentioned a long stay resident, a builder, who had been working on Mother Redcap's. Part of his work had been to fill in the well, which this account describes as "square and situated at the front of the house." He told Mrs Fisher that down the well were three entrances to tunnels. Some of the tunnels had caved in, but the one that ran to St Hilary's was intact. Another ran "under some nearby cottages" while the third was "believed to run somewhere via the docks to an old Birkenhead church, possibly the priory".

The nineteenth century writer James Stonehouse recorded having "been up the tunnels or caves at the Red and White Noses many a time for great distances," and how he "once … went up the caves for at least a mile, and could have gone further." He believed that they were "excavated by smugglers in part, and partly natural cavities of the earth." Elsewhere he records the tradition that "the caves at the Red Noses communicated in some way and somewhere with Mother Redcap's." Other accounts say that a second tunnel led from the Priory to Mother Redcap's. In 1897, "an old man who had explored them in his youth" was living at Wallasey,

The most famous of the caves, known as the Wormhole, lies beneath Rock Villa. The sea entrance was blocked off after the construction of the Promenade, but until recently, it could be entered via a manhole and a vertical ladder from the garden of the house. Formerly opened each year for charity, the cave consists of a narrow tunnel on a north-south axis, which opens out into a main cavern containing a well, and a bricked-up tunnel on the east wall. Several dates are carved on the walls, including one as early as 1619. The air is said to be fresh, even at the southern end, so there must be an outlet. Recent rumours, however, suggest that the owner has barred off the entrance.

It is said that the tunnel is linked with others in a cavern underneath the Palace Amusement Arcade in New Brighton. Tradition maintains that smugglers and wreckers concealed their booty in the cavern, which is sadly no longer accessible. The tunnels are believed to lead to Bidston, Mother Redcap's (from which another tunnel is supposed to lead to Birkenhead Priory), St Hilary's Church, and Fort Perch Rock. The existence of the Fort Perch Rock tunnel itself was confirmed by a geo-physical survey carried out in the mid-seventies, (at the same time as the one at Mother Redcap's) and it has been suggested that it was built as an escape route for the fort in case of attack. The cellars of the Palace itself consist of an extensive warren of tunnels that predate the current building by a substantial if uncertain period, being lined with handmade brick joined with cement rather than mortar.

The Old Palace and the Floral Pavilion were built in 1880, opening on Whit Monday the next year. It included an aquarium, baths, a theatre, a ballroom said to have been the finest in England, an aviary, and a zoo. During the construction of the original building, a pit was discovered which "revealed evidence that it had been used by smugglers and wreckers for the purpose of concealing their goods" and that possibly it hid something more sinister. A "sickening" stench emanated from the pit, and only the liberal use of disinfectants could eventually remove the contents so work could continue. According to local traditions, this is connected with the wreck of the Pelican in 1793. The cavern was transformed into an underground waterway known as The Grotto, where small boats could sail past illuminated caves. It extended for over 250 metres, and is said to have ended beneath the bottom of Rowson Street.

The passages are said to extend as far as St Hilary's, Leasowe Castle, and even Chester Castle. Although the latter seems highly, it is possible that the tunnel leading to St Hilary's joins up with one of the tunnels from beneath the Palace. Perhaps they are one and the same tunnel.

No tunnels are currently accessible from St Hilary's at the present date, and the vault beneath the old tower was covered by a tiled floor in the late nineteenth century. But according to the rector, Canon Paul Robinson, one of the parishioners remembers going down a tunnel in the thirties, below Swinton Old Hall, the site of the modern rectory, a few hundred years away from the old tower. Joseph Ruiz says that a well exists beneath the front sitting room of the old rectory, fifteen feet wide and 350 feet deep, and it is believed to lead to a tunnel; this is also mentioned in an article in the Wirral News. The article refers to a legend that says an underground passage leads from the rectory to the church (presumably the old tower) and then on to Mother Redcap's. According to legend, Mother Redcap's treasure – the missing prize money of the privateers - lies somewhere in this tangled labyrinth. But what happened to it? Is it lost forever? It is possible that some of the treasure has been found over the years.

Mother Redcap's death appears to have been during the Revolutionary and Napoleonic Wars. In about 1850, a "quantity of Spade Ace guineas was found in a cavity by the shore," which is the origin of the name Guinea Gap. The money dated from the late seventeenth to mid eighteenth century (William and Mary, George I and George II), and was found with a sword and a skeleton.

According to Joseph Ruiz, the Pioneer Corps employed a man named Morty Brightmore in 1942. One of his duties was to dig sand out of the Red Noses caves for use in sandbags. While so engaged, he found an old leather purse filled with gold coins, which he reported to the officer in charge of the operation. It is said that the officer gave the coins to a jeweller to be melted down to make a bracelet for his daughter.

In 1979, Bob Wadsworth, owner of the end house in Seymour Street, was clearing out his cellar when he found the entrance to a large tunnel beneath some bricks. The tunnel led in the direction of the sea. Investigating the tunnel, Bob found an old, rotten bag of silver coins, which he sold to local antique dealer Frank Upton for £3 and two packets of cigarettes. As is so often the case, the council later filled in the tunnel.

The current writer frequently found himself up against a brick wall – sometimes literally – as he struggled to uncover the truth behind these rumours. Tunnels had been blocked up as soon as they were discovered; the publication of

Joseph Ruiz's book apparently resulted in the blocking of all the Red Noses tunnel entrances; documents had mysteriously vanished from the reference sections of libraries whose staff were oddly brusque and unhelpful: finally, the writer was warned that all information on the subject had been suppressed by the local authority.

It remains an enigma.

7 MYTH AND LEGENDS – JACK O'
LEGS BY MARGARET ETHERIDGE

In Britain we are very fortunate to have a wealth of history, myths and legends - King Arthur and Merlin (Cornwall and Wales), Mother Redcap (Wirral), Robin Hood (Nottingham) and Jack O'Legs (Hertfordshire) to name but a few.

Jack O'Legs is perhaps the least well known of the few mentioned above. Jack is thought to have lived in the 14th century at a time in history that saw war, plague (the Black Death), and the first peasant revolt. Legend suggests that he was a similar character to the more well known Robin Hood, as like Robin Hood, Jack was a thief, robbing rich travellers, but was generous in giving to the poor. His favourite place for giving money to the poor is adjacent to the Great

North Road and is still referred to as 'Jack's Hill' to this day. It is said that Jack was a renowned archer, being able to shoot a straight arrow for three miles and having the skill to take down a bird at half a mile.

Jack lived in a cave in a wood at Weston (close to the village of Graveley near Stevenage) - the wood is not there any longer, but where the wood stood is still known as 'The Cave' and the neighbouring field is called 'Weston Wood'. Jack was an unusually tall man. There are two stones just inside the entrance to Holy Trinity Church, Weston, where Jack is buried marking the head and foot of his grave. Legend states that they are 14 feet (4.3 m) apart, though they are actually about 8 feet (2.4 m) apart. If this is accurate, this would make Jack one of the tallest people in history, hence him being called a giant. He was so tall, he often talked to his friends through their windows on the first floor, placing his elbows on the windowsill with ease.

Jack's end came one spring day when he came to Weston, finding the townsfolk worried. Their harvest had failed and they only had a small quantity of flower left. Jack knew of a miller in nearby Baldock, who had plenty of flour, went off to the Black Horse Mill at Baldock, and robbed a sack of flour. The flour didn't last long, so Jack had to make a return on more than one occasion to steal more flour.

At this time in history, bakers and millers were wealthy people and Jack's robberies didn't go unnoticed. So a group of millers and bakers decided that they would act and get rid of Jack. They waited in ambush for Jack behind the tombstones in the churchyard.

Fearing Jack's great strength, they let him pass by and clubbed him from behind, bound him tightly and burned out his eyes with a red-hot poker. At this point Jack made a last request as he sensed this was his end. He requested to be put out of his misery. He also requested, "I can't see to shoot you now and you have to bury me somewhere. Let me shoot towards home and bury me where my arrow falls." The bakers allowed Jack's request.

Jack's longbow was placed into his hands and, from where he was standing in Baldock churchyard, he took a great pull on the string, releasing the arrow swiftly in the direction of Weston. The arrow sailed over his cave and hit Weston church tower, over three miles away!

Source: Myths and Legends
(myths.e2bn.org/mythsandlegends/view_myth.php?id=37)
and Wikipedia-29.06.11.

8 THE WOZZLES BY JUSTINE ROBINSON

They are 30cm tall, in a variety of colours; each having a pair of shells about where their ears would be. These stand up to show how happy they are and point down when they are upset. Mischievous creatures who seek fun and laughter as much as they can, they are fed by a set of workers called Enchiers. Enchiers exist to cover the rock with moss and lichen which the creatures eat. They flavour the lichen and moss to encourage the creatures to eat as much as they can. At the moment it is stale socks, but a few weeks ago it was chocolate and bolognaise. The Enchiers are the opposite of the other creatures, as they are serious and work-driven.

9 A WOZZLE STORY – BAD MOOD DAY BY CAROLE WILSHAW

When a Wozzle wakes up in a bad mood, the bad mood spreads like flu. It very quickly spreads through a whole colony of Wozzles until everyone is feeling bad tempered and irritable. Wozzles do not snap out of bad moods easily and once a Wozzle is in a bad mood there is no point anyone else trying to do anything about it. They would much rather everyone shares the bad mood before anyone will cheer up. Clarice Wozzle had had her sleep disturbed because of loud snoring (a common problem with Wozzles).

By mid morning The Wronguns had called at the Wozzles' rock pool and on seeing the state of doom and gloom did nothing more than laugh. The Wronguns always did things the wrong way round and it was usually done to irritate whoever they were visiting - and it worked!

"No point staying around today." Leticia Wrongun remarked. "We might as well go back and find fault with someone else."

"Miserable lot!" moaned Jeremiah Wrongun. "They can't even be bothered to have a decent fight or wrestling match, they're so boring."

The Wozzles just stared at the Wronguns as they went off sniggering.

It then began raining and the rock pool, which started off with a nice little puddle at the bottom, started filling up. The Wozzles didn't feel like swimming so they had to clamber up the rock side to find somewhere to sit. After a while, it stopped raining and the Wozzles were debating if it was time for a dip in the pool. Their conversation was disturbed by the distant sound of clanging of metal.

"Here we go," announced Manzoni Wozzle, "that sounds like Zachary Brown and his missus on their way."

Zachary Brown was a lighthouse keeper and even in his spare time, he looked for people to rescue.

"No doubt they'll be bringing Dorothy Parrot," Woodwedge Wozzle grumbled.

"And Chbick that grumpy guinea pig," added Clarice.

"And not forgetting that silly fish, Blurt- he always comes."

"It's not Blurt – it's called Blurtrem." Clarice corrected Woodwedge.

"Well, whatever it's called, it's spoilt rotten, that fish is."

The Wozzles were right - the clanging noise was Zachary accompanied by his lady friend, Blythe Dinga, carrying their picnic table and chairs across the rocks. Zachary appeared, in his squelching wellington boots, and Blythe with the goldfish. They were followed closely by the guinea pig and by the parrot (who was dragging one foot and one wing).

"That parrot walks like a pirate, doesn't it?" said Clarice, "Do you think there's something wrong with his leg and his wing?"

"Nah!" said Manzoni Wozzle, "If you watch - when Zachary and his missus isn't around it doesn't limp at all – it's just pretending."

Blythe was not in a good mood and was nagging Zachary for bringing his telescope. Zachary was in a bad mood because of Blythe's nagging and he was grumbling at her for bringing the goldfish. They set up the table and chairs next to the rock pool. Blythe sat down and painted her chipped finger nails with pink varnish. Zachary got out his telescope and looked out to sea to see if he could find people to rescue.

Meanwhile the Wozzles were having their swim in the rock pool. They splashed about a bit and were just starting to feel a little better when

PLONK! Something landed in the water. It was Blurtrem the fish. Blythe had let it out for a swim. The Wozzles didn't like fish much - especially ones that occupied the same rock pool as them - so they all clambered out of the water and sat on the rocks again to watch the fat, orange, scaly thing doing circuits of their swimming pool.

Blythe took the tea cups and plates from the hamper and set them out on the table. She then placed her home made cup cakes and doughnuts on the cake stand and poured the tea for Zachary and herself. Blythe offered Zachary a cup cake but quite suddenly he jumped up from the table knocking over the cakes, most of which rolled off the table and onto the rocks.

"Got to go," shouted Zachary, "rescue at sea - drowning out there - look"

"Where?" said Blythe, not really interested.

"There - look - they're waving at us - they want me to rescue them."

Zachary hurried off to get his rowing boat from the old wooden post where it was moored further down the beach. He was soon on his way, rowing out across the waves to reach the marooned party. Blythe was left with the remains of the picnic. She sat and waited for a while but when Zachary didn't return she packed up the table and chairs and hamper and went home followed by Chbick and by Dorothy (who was still dragging its leg and one wing).

"Oh no!" squealed Clarice looking into the pool, "she's gone and left the fish behind!"

"And those cakes – look, they're rolling towards the pool," shouted Woodwedge.

Blythe had completely forgotten Blurtrem who was still circling the pool, oblivious to the fact that it was now filling up with expanding cake sponge. The Wozzles watched as Blurtrum slowly became invisible within a mass of soggy sponge.

Blurtrum surfaced for air a couple of times looking very lemon and chocolaty - giving him a sort of all over marbled effect.

"What are we going to do now?" cried Clarice.

"We could leave him," said Manzoni.

"No, we can't do that – we've got to get him out somehow."

"Look! He's drowning."

"Don't be stupid, goldfish don't drown."

"He's drowning in cake sponge!"

All the Wozzles were now lined up around the pool and the Wronguns had come back to see what the commotion was about.

Troikle Wozzle, who had been watching the developing situation from the top of the rocks, shouted to the others, "Throw him that doughnut."

"Whatever for?" cried Woodwedge.

"So he can hang on to it - like a rubber ring."

"Make a seaweed rope, quickly," shouted Troikle.

The Wozzles worked together to make a long rope of seaweed and tied one end to the doughnut.

At the top of the rocks, the little group of Wronguns were sniggering and pointing at the choking goldfish below but they did not offer to help. The Wozzles threw the doughnut to Blurtrem who flipped himself through it, ready to be hauled out. As the Wozzles began to pull on the rope there was suddenly a shriek from Troikle.

"Quick! Hide! Daft Things approaching!"

"We can't - we can't let go of the fish," shouted Wedgewood.

"Take cover but hang on to the rope."

"What about Blurt?"

"Push him under that bit of rock that's sticking out and then hide yourself."

"Quick! They're coming!"

The Wozzles tucked the fish, and then themselves, around the rock sides under a precipice out of harm's way. Everyone held tightly onto the seaweed rope.

The Daft Things (consisting of Zachary and his rescued party) were all laughing and joking as they went past – squelching and slipping over the rocks pools in their flip flops and plastic crocs. They avoided the rock pool, pulling odd faces and making strange noises of disgust about the state of it and how terrible it was, 'people leaving litter behind'.

With the Daft Things out of the way, the Wozzles set to work again to hoist Blurtrem from the sponge cake pool. Another party by this time had surrounded the pool – it was the Tronches. The Tronches stood with the Wronguns and stared in disbelief at the lemon and chocolate coloured fish hanging on to a doughnut.

"Right!" ordered Troikle, "Continue rescue - one two three – PULL!"

The Wozzles dragged the doughnut with Blurtrem pathetically flopped over it, slowly up the rocks.

"What a sight you look, Blurt!" commented Woodwedge as the fish slithered past her.

"Blurtrem!" gargled the fish, "I'm Blurtrem not Blurt."

Woodwedge found the fish's bowl so she could put him back in but Troikle thought it would be a good idea to hose him down first by using the Tronches who always got rid of un-necessary water by spurting it from their ears. The Tronches did as Troikle asked and before long Blurtrem was restored to his normal orange colour.

A few feet away, Zachary was saying goodbye to the Daft Things. When they had gone, he looked around him as though still expecting to see Blythe sitting at the picnic table.

"Humph!" He scratched his head and then looked through his telescope to see if he could see Blythe. He couldn't see her at all but he did find Blurtrem who was now doing fast circuits round his bowl. "What are you doing here, Blurtrem," he said, "all on your own?"

With that, he picked up the bowl and off home he went.

The Wronguns and the Tronches had left as well and the Wozzles decided that they must move to another rock pool.

"Let's take that cherry that fell off the cup cake," said Manzoni, "we can have a game of football when we get there."

Troikle kicked it and it landed a good way off. By the time the Wozzles had caught up with it, the seagulls Merle and Hoult had beaten them to it. They had the cherry in their beaks and they were squabbling over it.

"I told you - it's a beach ball," squawked Merle.

"I told you it's not – it's a cherry and you can eat it," hissed Hoult.

"You can't eat a beach ball"

"It's not a beach ball, it's a ...

And with that, the cherry split in two and both seagulls fell backwards with a lot of squawking and flapping about.

"I told you never to listen to that parrot," hissed Hoult. "She distinctly told me it was a cherry."

"WELL! She distinctly told ME it was beach ball," Merle snapped back.

The argument continued and the Wozzles blamed Troikle for kicking the ball so hard. Clarice and Woodwedge were just fed up with everyone but Woodwedge did try to find something good about the day.

"Well, at least we saved Blurt," she said

"BLUTREM!" yelled Manzoni and Clarice.

The End

10 WITNESS FOR THE DEFENCE BY JUSTINE ROBINSON

Edward Burrington (Teddy) looked up from the bench towards the defendant. She sat as meek as meek could be, her bleached streak hair braided into two lengths which draped to her shoulder blades, the tips dipped into a vivid turquoise dye which was gently fading.

Tatine Beryl Gupchek gently rotated the wad of chewing gum around her mouth, occasionally interrupting the pattern to smack down on the glob of gum producing a sound like a two year old hitting their bath water. She was charged with shoplifting, an offence usually dealt with a caution, a fine, and a severe looking at. But Tatine was a persistent offender and the shop had decided to take the case further. She appeared to have been scrubbed to within an inch of her life. The teardrop tattoo by her left eye was the only mark on her alabaster skin. Her clothes while being respectable were obviously fresh from a charity shop. The clash of the colours and the patterns was enough to hurt a person's eyes.

Tatine had declared that she was not guilty. The shop Try Before You Buy had provided CCTV footage of a scantily clad, big haired female slipping jewellery and other objects into concealed pockets as well as into a large carryall she was toting about. The transcript of the initial search was interesting. One, because throughout the procedure Tatine had only spoken to give her name and her address; the second interesting thing in the transcript was the amount of goods retrieved.

At the club, when persuading Teddy to become a magistrate, Chad Cringleworth had hinted that it was a fascinating role to have. Up until this case, he would have challenged what exactly Chad classed as fascinating. Teddy looked at the defence brief and pitied him. He looked to his right and would swear that Aganetha Wright-White was asleep. And to his left Alex Jacksun was playing on her or his iPhone. Teddy had been intrigued by Alex, who was either a masculine female or a feminine male. She/he did not mingle with the bench and there was no indication of his or her true name.

The defence brief stood with a cowered hesitancy that warned of an early escape to the golf links. "I call Camilla Ulrika Valentina Gupchek to the stand." Teddy looked up. this suddenly was interesting.

A divine epitome of divaness sashayed to the box. The haze of perfume and powder followed this seemingly magnificent woman. She adjusted her skirt and fitted blouse before perching on the seat. She assessed the bench, dismissed Aganetha, was confused by Alex, and turned her attention on Teddy. The downdraft of her eyelashes alone was enough to sweep the aroma of her perfume all around her. She offered a simpering smile, just the correct mix of coy and sex. Then turned to face the defence brief, who seemed to blush under her direct stare. He started with a hesitancy suddenly developing a stammer, which he did not have. "M m m s. Gupchek." Now the court were all transfixed between the two of them. "You have stated a desire to speak in the defence of Tatine V."

Camilla issued a purring trill of laughter. "Ooh, George! Call me Camilla as we are here. Ms indeed. You'll give me airs!" With that she turned, giving Tatine a look that could only be described as loving before turning to face the full court, the magistrates, the clerk and everyone sat in on the case. Kimberly Vert, the owner of Try Before You Buy, shuddered, as she was aware of what she was about to witness. Camilla now had the floor, so she began.

"To look on Tatina is to look on the face of innocence." Teddy and Alex both looked at the defendants and were both struck by the teardrop tattoo. They looked at each other shrugged and watched the unfolding soap drama. "Her devoted mother is serving out the last of her sentence at Askham Grange. Except that Meme is not her mother and I am not her sister but her Aunt. her mum is Chastity, my youngest sister, who at the moment is held on charges of extortion regarding sexual acts in Spain." Camilla thrilled to see the looks of befuddlement. She looked to Tatine and saw no surprise on her face. She knew the girl was sharp and could have worked things out.

"Tatine is a good girl. I've a stack of report cards from male teachers delighting in her presence in their class. In fact, I've three letters requesting that the family implore with the school to place Tatine in their form class. Mr Brown would have been prepared to come to testify except the fact his wife has banned him having any contact with her, unless he is prepared to lose parts of his body.

"I looked at the CCTV footage and failed to see any resemblance to the girl I know. We were raised as sisters. I know she would not risk capture for some trinkets. If they had been selling Pandora bracelets then things might have been different," she stopped to shimmy to make sure that her chest and impressive cleavage was displayed to its best. The engineering required to produce such a canyon did not come cheap and should be viewed. "Our mutual gentleman friend lauds us with gold and stones out of gratitude so Tatine has no need to steal." She stopped for a breath then carried on "What sort of name is Try Before You Buy? It seems to encourage using and walking away. My brother Dwayne's Sharice says that she wouldn't look twice at the stuff. And the woman is an avarice magpie so if she says no it tells you a lot about the shop. Tatine is the only one of us who finished school without time off to give birth. She is as she said innocent."

With that, Camilla slinked out of the witness stand, blew a kiss to Tatine, and oozed over to the bench. Standing in front of Teddy, she delved into her cleavage and extracted a contact card, which she handed to him. Stopping and appraising Alex philosophically, she handed him/her one of her cards as well. Suggestively sucking her left pointing finger, she made to leave the court.

The defence called out. "Camilla, you have to take questions from the prosecution." Pouting, that her performance had been interrupted, she stomped back to the stand. The prosecution declined the opportunity to ask any questions. This time when she made her exit, she presented him with her contact card and a kiss, which left a perfect set of scarlet lip imprints on his cheek.

The bench left with the legal clerk to reach their conclusion. They returned within fifteen minutes. They would have returned within five minutes but had had to explain to Aganetha all that had happened.

Teddy took the centre seat and addressed the room. Tatine looked up and for the first time. "After reviewing the evidence and the testimony we find Tatine Beryl Gupchek guilty of repeated theft from Try Before You Buy. We sentence her to four month in prison suspended for three years. We also fine her two hundred pounds, and order that she completes one hundred hours of community payback."

"Bonza. Ta, you worships. I needed a new fella and you only get the best in payback. I love youse." Her voice was a shrill gutter voice filled with missed letters and harsh accents. She left and made to leave, yelling as she ran "Hey,

Cam, I thought you'd screwed it up. But I got the payback so I can select a new fella. Thanks chuck." She reached Camilla who was just handing out a calling card to a security guard. They left arm in arm.

The Court reporter sat transfixed; you couldn't make it up. It was a shame to waste this he would case in the "Look who's in court" column but when writing his novel have a fantastic source to use.

11 LABOUR BY JOHN HOYLAND

Cecil loved his job. Twelve hours a day, six days a week, he worked at the factory he had worked at since he left school. There was no more conscientious employer than our Cecil. He was always on time, never absent, never late, never took a day off sick. When he wasn't at work, he was at his allotment, digging up soil, turning the muck over with his hands. He loved the feel of the dark rich soil as he trickled it between his fingers and broke up the clods of earth with his hands. He thought of the generations before him who had worked this land and he felt connected to it as if he too were some exotic greenhouse plant that had been transplanted and blossomed, thrusting forth its brilliant new shoots to the light.

On Saturday night, he walked into The Bird in Hand a sober man and walked out of it at ten o'clock, so intoxicated he felt one step nearer to

God. Drunk he gazed at the stars as they danced in a sky that seemed to swirl in a kaleidoscope of swirling light above his head and he was at peace with himself. On Sunday morning, he went to church and prayed to God for forgiveness and then went and drank his local form of communion wine, a pint of best, at the pub. Then he stumbled home and ate his dinner and fell asleep in some fossil of an old armchair like a giant in the seven sleepers den.

The Gandi Belt factory had been at the bottom of the embankment as long as he could remember. High stone walls stood around the workshops where over a thousand men worked on machines day and night. Little windows like apertures looked down from a turret at the corner of a factory wall that looked to his young eyes like a tall tower in some Arthurian castle. Light shimmered through misted panes of rainbow glass bending blues and greys; leaving glittering pools that filtered through the branches of a nearby tree, cascading in a leaf-fall at his feet. Cecil imagined that he was a prince, come from some distant land to save a princess who would let down her long flowing hair for him to climb up and rescue her.

This was where adventures were born. Then the land of work was still a place of mystery. Here, he thought, boys became men and moved out into the world dreaming that they might achieve great things. All was possible, his father taught him, if only you put your back into it. Work would become the pinnacle of his days, the map and compass of his passing life. He had walked past the factory everyday when he was still at school, and heard the great roar from the machinery within, and heard the whistle blow, like some huge leviathan crying out, for change of shift. Clouds of steam gushed out of the earth as the chimneys, like gargantuan blow-holes, belched forth fire and smoke. He loved to watch the men as they came out cursing and swearing, carrying their wages on a Friday night. This was the life, he thought, when you became a man.

He too would be proud of the sweat he wore that like engine oil, smoothed the muscles and bones of you working body as it struggled with tasks that stretched the fibre of you to the limit. Work defined who you were and replaced your passport as a form of identification. You were a stoker, or a belt man, a breaker, or a foreman, and you shared in the fellowship of labour with your fellow workers and passed round the common drinking mug like a holy chalice.

His father had taught him that there was a sort of nobility in the working life. Self-educated, and a sort of workingman's Ruskin he read his bible and he read his Karl Marx and between the two he cobbled together his own personal gospel and his own road to salvation. "Nobody should tell you what to think," he had once told his son. "Be your own man and beholden to nobody else and never forget your as best as the next." For Tobias there were only two men who ranked higher, 'God and the King.' No other governor commanded the kind of respect bestowed on these two creatures and in life he never pulled his forelock or bowed to any man, least of all his boss at the old firm.

Madge was his soul mate. Cecil had met her at a local dance when he was sixteen. He was such a fine looking man she thought, tall, a mite over six feet with a thick bush of red hair that looked like the flame that Moses saw in the burning bush. His mates called him Ginger and despite his large frame he had a poise and grace all of his own and a sensitivity when he sat and listened to you as if you were the only person in the room. He looked older and wiser than he was like some kind of prophet as he held her hand and talked politics or love to her. It was all one and the same to her. She loved to hear him speak.

They were married two years later at the local registry office and rented a small two up and down in Oakbridge Road, then part of a new working class area. It was a natty little house with rose bushes at the front and seven feet of garden at the back, and behind that, the alley that ran between the rows of houses. It was still gas lighting then and at night the lamps would be turned on and each one lit up the street and surrounding fields with a blue shimmer that looked like some ghoulish firework as it shone on the faces of the men as they came home from work and the women who waited for them at the end of the path.

They had been together for eighteen months when Madge became pregnant. It was not an easy pregnancy. She was always sickly and never seemed to have much of an appetite. There was a dispute at the factory over new machinery that had been installed and for the first time in his life, Cecil was home before five-0-clock in the evening. He used this spare time to decorate the small back bedroom as a nursery for their little girl, he was sure the child would turn out a girl.

One bitterly cold January morning Madge's waters broke. Cecil sitting by her in bed, got up and in his stockingless feet walked down to the kitchen and filling the big copper pans with water put them on the gas ring to boil. Walking out the front door, he just remembered at the last moment he had nothing on his feet, he went back upstairs for his slippers, and wrapping a dressing gown around him, he walked the seventy yards to the telephone at the junction of Oakbridge Road and Poulton Way. On the way to the public telephone box, he left a slipper in the snow, and only when he had phoned the doctor did he realise that his left foot was coated in a thin veneer of white icing.

Around Oakbridge Road was still semi rural then, with fields that ran down Gorsehill Crescent down a step hill that surfaced behind the Gandi factory like a humpback whale. There was a large house on the corner that looked towards the bridges and if you turned left at the base of the sharp rise in the road, you walked down a winding path until you reached the old ferry. Cecil, unaware of the fine snow that clung to his lips and to his eyelashes and hair set off for home. There was an alarm bell sounding somewhere inside his head and a small voice that was telling him 'hurry, hurry on home, as fast, fast, fast as you can.'

His toes were blue and the sole of his foot so cold with clumps of snow clinging to the tips of his nails. A cold chill ran through him like lightning and it was as if a winter wind coursing through his heart had deposited icicles in his arteries and frozen the currents of blood inside his chest into glaciers. 'Something is not quite right' he told himself as he looked at Madge and her pale face and blue lips as the ambulance appeared in the street. "Better to be safe," Dr Hoppins had told him, trying to reassure and provide comfort but Cecil knew there was more in it than that.

Myra was born some twelve hours later. There had been complications and she had been born with the cord wrapped around her neck. Madge had lost a great deal of blood and needed a transfusion and even after she came out of hospital could not get out of bed for several days. Myra was a chunky little baby with a thick mop of dark hair, fat rotund little arms and legs that could have supported a Victorian chaise lounge. Cecil was won over by her completely and would rush home from work to hold her in his arms.

And so the three of them lived together and day followed day. Myra was a healthy child and hardly ever sick. Most days she played out in the back with the local boys preferring their company than the girls in the road who only wanted to play with dolls.

She adored her father and wanted to be like him, and yearned to be tall and strong. No boy would ever hurt her and when one day Tommy Smith, grabbed her by her hair she picked up a brick and hit him with it, knocking out two of his front teeth and nearly breaking his jaw.

The next day she got a pair of scissors and cut her hair short. "Oh Myra look what you've done with your hair" her mother exclaimed bitterly. "Well," Myra responded, defiantly casting the locks hair onto the flames of their coal fire, "no boy will ever be able to pull my pigtails again." Cecil was saddened by the loss of his precious darlings golden curls but Myra saw it as her first kind of moral victory and proof that whatever the cost she would make it in a man's world.

One afternoon she had sat around all day when she had come across an old scarred wooden sea chest in her parents rooms. Opening it up she came across letters and old photographs and most wonderful of all, books. Picking one up, she looked at the title 'Uncle Tom's Cabin'. She turned the first page over and slowly began to read.

Myra possessed a hungry mind and this treasure chest of books proved to be a place of refuge and safety away from a hostile world. It was hard work at first and she often came over words she had never encountered before or lost her place in the narrative. Yet as she read about Tom and his silent courage, fighting the evils of slavery like a Christian warrior, she was filled with hope and a belief that she too might one day achieve great things. When she came to Tom's death and read of his suffering, she felt a tightening inside of her and a release as she sobbed as if she would never stop crying. She did not know that it could be this way, that words like powerful spells could possess you and change the way you saw things as if you saw them through a magic mirror.

She yearned to be the hero of her own life. She did not want to sit around in any enchanted tower, waiting to be rescued. She wanted to fight the good fight and battle demons and monsters. She wanted to be Don Quixote, David Copperfield, Christian following the path to the city of salvation. She to could be Captain Scott, Kitchener of Khartoum, Lawrence of Arabia and nothing seemed impossible and no goal seemed beyond her grasp.

That summer, when she turned eight, the world turned upside down. War was the only subject neighbours seemed to talk about. It was coming and times would change and places and people would never be the same again. The bombs were falling and it was not safe for children who lived close to the docks and the large ships and so she was parcelled off to the countryside where she would be safe. Years later she recalled standing at Lime Street Station, a card hung around her neck with her name printed out on it in large crayoned letters, carrying her gas mask and a small suitcase with one change of clothes, a few books and some sandwiches wrapped in waxed paper.

Sitting on the train as it pulled out of the station she caught a glimpse of her mother and thought how could she bear to give me away. Yet as the tracks vanished into a mysterious distance and she travelled out of the city and saw fields and trees she told herself that this could be the start of a great adventure. This was how events unfolded themselves in the stories she read and she would be changed forever. She was travelling beyond where dragons lived, beyond the edges of the earth and she would meet such brave new creatures who talked in magical ways.

What Myra most desired was freedom of mind, to be able to think her own thoughts, to shape her own story. Back at home, she often felt confined, locked in some damp basement within. She believed that somewhere she could find a key to release all she believed herself capable of becoming and that one day this would happen and she would find true happiness. Yet her lips tightened and she retreated back into this dark place when she stepped down from the train and was confronted by the towering castle-like shape of Mrs Braddocks, the wife of the farmer, conscripted to look after her.

Mrs Braddocks had such a large mouth and giant hands with thick fingers that wanted to choke you. Mrs Braddocks had such a loud voice and there was nowhere to go to escape from this booming foghorn and she carried such a heavy, stout stick that itched to hit you and any moment you expected her to call out fee fi fo fum and swallow you whole as if you were some tasty morsel in a pie. She would pierce you on the tip of a monstrous fork and you would disappear down her huge cavern of a throat and never be seen again. She did not think there would be any kind stranger passing by, who would hear her cries and with one chop of his axe split open the enormous mountain of a belly that Mrs Braddocks carried before her, and so release her from this dark gastric cave into the air and sunlight.

Grabbing her by the arm and hauling her behind, as if Myra were some sort of anchor, they sailed on down a winding lane where branches overhung dark shadows like ships masts reeling in a squall. Sometimes the sun shattered through the green canopy and Myra was blinded until they stepped back into shade and the darkness closed in. Then coming around a bend, there stood the house, with a wild weeping willow leaning over a hedge, its long coils of leafy hair reaching out, its trunk bending in a breeze. The house itself was made out of white chocolate with rough cast slabs of cake for walls and flakes of darker straw for a thatched roof. This was a house even Hansel and Gretel would have devoured. It seemed a perfect picture post-card of delight. Yet the ivy around the window frames gave off a bitter smell as if something inside the house had gone off and the door hinges growled as they entered a darker hall.

"Go on girl, get to your room," bawled Mrs Braddocks. "Top of the stairs and third door on the right." Like a prisoner walking to her cell, Myra took each step by step and slowly made her way up. Flowers on the wall-paper, like faces, glanced down with compassion, as she passed by. Then slumping by a small iron bed that looked like it belonged to the smallest of the three bears, Myra covered her face with her linked hands, and as if praying fervently, she solemnly bowed her head and shed some silent tears.

ABOUT THE AUTHORS

Margaret Etheridge moved to Wirral from Hertfordshire some 36 years ago, but was born in Carmarthen, South Wales - the same birth place as King Arthur's Merlin. This connection was Margaret's inspiration to write about Merlin and develop an interest in all things mythical and legendary.

Justine Robinson says, "Reading inspires me to share my enjoyment with others. Writing should bemuse, amuse, and enthuse readers to read more. My passion is for the historic period of the Knights Templar, and following the traditions of that time, I write to entertain, whether with exciting pieces which evoke memories of a mischievous past, or the intrigue of crime writing. The power of words encourages me always to read different genres and to attempt to write pieces that make anyone reading consider the fifteen minutes or so they spend as time well spent."

Carole Wilshaw was born in Coventry and studied Design and Illustration at Lanchester Polytechnic in the 1970s. She moved to the Wirral in 1989 after living and working in London, Scotland and Leicestershire. Carole has taught Calligraphy and Illustration in Adult Education for many years. She has two grown up children and currently works as a learning mentor in Further Education. When not working, Carole enjoys writing poetry, short stories and travel articles, writing and illustrating stories for children, walking her dogs and catching up with friends and family.

Sheila Perry *says "I live on the Wirral and I am a keen walker and member of the Ramblers Association, after attending a Creative Writing Course with tutor Gavin Chappell I was inspired to write some local walks and draw and paint illustrations. I am fortunate to have so much beauty nature and history right on my doorstep"*

John Hoyland *is married with four grown-up children and three grandchildren. He was born and has lived in Wallasey most of his life. A registered nurse retired due to ill health, he has been involved in writing since he was about eight years of age. He currently works part time in a second hand book shop in Liscard and describes himself as a "prolific reader and book buyer."*

Gavin Chappell *has been involved in writing and editing for the last decade. He has written and edited short stories, translations, poetry, novels and non-fiction. Also a qualified teacher of further education, Gavin has taught English and Creative Writing for several years. He is editor of Schlock! Webzine (www.schlock.co.uk)*

Printed in Great Britain
by Amazon